What Baptists Believe

and

Why They Believe It

By

J. G. BOW, D.D.

ISBN: 0-8054-9104-X

4291-04

THE SUNDAY SCHOOL BOARD
OF THE SOUTHERN BAPTIST CONVENTION
Nashville, Tennessee

WHAT BAPTISTS BELIEVE

CHAPTER I

The Absolute Authority of the Inspired Scriptures

"We believe the Holy Bible was written by men divinely inspired, and is a perfect treasure of heavenly instruction; that it has God for its Author, salvation for its end, and truth, without any mixture of error for its matter; that it reveals the principles by which God will judge us; and, therefore is, and shall remain to the end of the world, the true basis of all Christian union, and the supreme standard by which all human conduct, creeds, and opinions should be tried."

Perhaps someone will say, Well, if there is any one thing upon which all claiming to be Christians are agreed, it is the authority of the Bible. Because of this very thing, namely, their professed agreement, and their actual disagreement, about the authority of the Scriptures, this article is written.

The Romanists have put tradition and papal authority not only upon an equality, but even above the Word of God, and by their traditions make the commandments of God of none effect. Through papal infallibility and church authority, they claim not only the right to change the ordinances as Christ instituted them, but, exercising that assumed authority, they have changed them, and even teach a changed condition of salvation, so that even the salvation of the soul depends not upon the power and will of God, but upon union with and obedience to themselves. They have even built an imaginary purgatory to scare their victims and filch from them their hard earnings.

Others following in their wake, have *assumed* and *inferred* very many things of which the Scriptures are ominously silent; feasts and fasts, church days and dogmas, offices and ordinances, which are not only unscriptural but antiscriptural. "Is it not for this cause that ye err, that ye know not the scriptures, nor the power of God" (Mark 12:24, ASV).

In a noted conference of ministers, composed of various denominations in Chicago, the chairman being a pedobaptist, a Catholic priest was invited to read a paper before the body. He stated that some things were necessary to salvation which the Bible did not enjoin—referring perhaps to penance, prayers for the dead, and other things which the Catholic church had added to the Word of God. To this the chairman objected. The priest replied, "Then you must give up your infant baptism, for the Bible knows nothing of any such ceremony; it rests solely on the authority of the Catholic Church by which it was introduced and established." Baptists believe the Bible is an all-sufficient rule of faith and practice.

Baptists still believe with Paul, that "Every scripture inspired of God is also profitable for teaching, for reproof, for correction, for instruction which is in righteousness: that the man of God may be complete, furnished completely unto every good work" (2 Tim. 3:16-17 ASV).

No one has a right to cull and cut, pervert, and reject to build up a system according to his own fancy.

We accept the Bible as God's Word. What it teaches is right, what it enjoins we must do, what it prohibits we must not do. By this Bible all human conduct, creeds, and opinions are to be tried. God's Word, like himself, is eternal and unchangeable.

"Though we, or an angel from heaven, preach any other gospel unto you than that which we have preached unto you, let him be accursed. . . . If any man preach any other gospel unto you than that ye have received, let him be accursed" (Gal. 1:8-9). "If any man teach otherwise, and consent not to wholesome words, even the words of our Lord Jesus Christ, and to the doctrine which is according to godliness; he is proud, knowing nothing, but doting about questions and strifes of words, whereof cometh envy, strife, railings, evil surmisings, perverse disputings of men of corrupt minds, and destitute of the truth, supposing that gain is godliness: from such withdraw thyself" (1 Tim. 6:3-5).

For these principles Baptists have been subjected to almost every conceivable form of torture and persecution.

The wise man said, "Buy the truth and sell it not." Our fathers have bought and presented these truths for us at a great price—the price of life and liberty, and for their sakes endured bitter poverty and vile persecutions. They were transmitted and committed to us, and it ill becomes us to barter them for the praise of their enemies.

The advocate of modern liberalism bids to sell principles he never possessed for a popularity he never deserved. Many re lavishly liberal with the things of God. No man can be more liberal than the Bible and be true to Christ. The less principle a man has the more liberal he can be with truth and sacred things.

We believe the declaration of the risen Saviour. "For I testify unto every man that heareth the words of the prophecy of this book, If any man shall add unto these things, God shall add unto him the plagues that are written in this book: and if any man shall take away from the words of the book of this prophecy, God shall take away his part out of the book of life, and out of the holy city, and from the things which are written in this book" (Rev. 22:18-19).

Hence no human power or ecclesiastical authority can alter or change this divine revelation. Any substitution or change of doctrine, ordinance, government, or condition of salvation is not only a sacrilege; but it is dishonoring to God and ruinous to souls. They cannot "add to," nor "take away." Jesus Christ is the "head over all things to the church." "There is one law-giver, who is able to save and to destroy."

How dare anyone to acknowledge that the Word of God teaches or commands one thing, and then say, "It matters not, something else will do just as well"! Will not the Master say, "Why call ye me Lord, Lord and do not the things which I say?" He has said, "If ye love me, keep my commandments." All who are *true* Baptists believe in the absolute, supreme, unchangeable authority of the inspired Scriptures.

CHAPTER II

The Atonement

Baptists believe in the atonement made by Christ as the only basis of salvation, the only means of reconciliation, the only ground of justification. Man is by nature a sinner, guilty, condemned, lost, and but for the atonement made by Christ, helpless and hopeless.

God is holy and just and must punish sin, is Almighty and able to punish sin; he cannot lie and has said that sin shall be punished. But God is also merciful; hence a willing, all-sufficient substitute is provided, and Jesus "bore our sins in his own body." God "made him to be sin for us, who knew no sin, that we might be made the righteousness of God in him." "Who gave himself a ransom for all, to be testified in due time." "Being justified fully by his grace through the redemption that is in Christ Jesus: whom God hath set forth to be a propitiation through faith in his blood, to declare his righteousness for the remission of sins that are past, through the forbearance of God, to declare, I say, at this time his righteousness: that he might be just, and the justifier of him which believeth in Jesus." The law is not made void, but through faith we establish the law. Jesus kept, made honorable, magnified and satisfied the law, becoming our accepted substitute; his righteousness, his right-doing, is imputed to us by faith and so we through him have kept the law. He took the sinner's place, bore his sins, met the penalty, and offers the sinner a child's place, and lets the sinner who trusts him go free.

Justice is not bribed nor cheated but fully sustained, and God is still just though he justifies the believer in Christ. Because Jesus has rendered perfect satisfaction by his life and atoning sacrificial death, God says, "If we confess our sins, he is faithful and just to forgive us our sins, and to cleanse us from all unrighteousness." Here is the sinner's only hope, Jesus and his atonement, "In whom we have redemption through his blood, the forgiveness of sins."

He must not, dares not, trust anything else—his penance, church, baptism, the Lord's Supper, not even his repentance and faith, but only Jesus. Baptists believe that no man cometh to God except through Jesus Christ.

> Venture on him, venture freely,
> Let no other trust intrude.
> None but Jesus, none but Jesus,
> Can do helpless sinners good.

CHAPTER III

Salvation

Prof. Wm. H. Whitsitt was once lecturing on Baptist History. He said: "The Baptists in other days had many trials, persecutions and discouragements; they also had some peculiarities, some of them had 'Foot-washing,' some of them had the 'Jerks,' but the best thing they had was—*religion.*"

Baptists hold and believe very many important truths, but the most important thing to every individual is the personal salvation of the soul. The most important work for Christians is the salvation of others. For this brings the greatest joy to them, the greatest of all blessings to those saved, and they glorify God in bearing fruit.

What Baptists believe is not from denominational pride, much less bigotry, narrowness, or selfishness. We seek to teach the truth through which God has ordained to save men and women.

Any departure from truth is error. Error can only do harm, not good. We are not allowed to change "the truth of God into a lie," not even for popularity or convenience.

How could anyone suppose that Baptists would hold to a doctrine which was so unpopular with other denominations and the world, so uncongenial to depraved human nature, from any selfishness or bigotry? Are we not human? Do we not love to be popular and please our fellow men? Ah! but, "We ought to obey God rather than men." It matters little what men think of us, but it is of infinite importance as to what God thinks of us.

Baptists believe that man is dead, depraved, blind, guilty, condemned, lost, and helpless, and, but for the grace of God in Christ Jesus, hopelessly so. "Dead in trespasses and sins." "Because we thus judge, that if one died for all, then were all dead" (2 Cor. 5:14).

Depraved means wicked, corrupt, vitiated. What do we mean by the expression "total depravity"? Does it mean total wickedness? God said, "There is none righteous, no, not one." Paul, proving that all were alike under sin in an unregenerate condition, says, "For we have before proved both Jews and Gentiles, that they are all under sin. As it is written, There is none righteous, no, not one: there is none that understandeth, there is none that seeketh after God. They are all gone out of the way." (See Romans 3:9-12.)

We do not mean that man is as bad as a demon, or as bad as he can be. You may put a drop of gall into a glass of water, and that water, all of it, is bitter, vitiated, corrupt, and unfit for drink. Not as bitter as it could be made, but it is all bitter. So every man, all the man, is depraved, sinful, corrupt. "The heart is deceitful above all things and desperately wicked." You may reiterate till the day of your death that you don't believe it, but the fact remains the same. God who knows the heart said it. "Unto them that are defiled and unbelieving is nothing pure; but even their mind and conscience is defiled" (Titus 1:15).

Blind—"In whom the God of this world hath blinded the minds of them which believe not." "But the natural man receiveth not the things of the Spirit of God: for they are foolishness unto him: neither can he know them, because they are spiritually discerned" (1 Cor. 2:14). "Having the understanding darkened, being alienated from the life of God through the ignorance that is in them, because of the blindness of their heart" (Eph. 4:18). "And all the world may become guilty before God" (Rom. 3:19).

Now we gladly believe that God has graciously made provision for the salvation of the irresponsible—the infant and the idiot—not because of what they have done but only through his mercy and grace in Jesus Christ. No duties are enjoined upon the irresponsible, no commandments are given unto them, no requirements are made of them. They are not subjects of gospel address.

We believe every responsible soul, which is unregenerate, impenitent, unbelieving, is lost—no matter how must we love them, nor how lovable they may be. They are lost now, not just in danger of being lost after a while. "He that believeth not is condemned already, because he hath not believed in the name of the only begotten Son of God" (John 3:18). But listen to the good news—the blessed gospel: "For God so loved the world, that he gave his only begotten Son, that whosoever believeth in him should not perish, but have everlasting life" (John 3:16). Yes, "whosoever believeth in him."

> **Pardon sweet, at His feet, ever free,**
> **Precious blood, like a flood, flows to me;**
> **Come to Him, Oh! come and live,**
> **For so freely He'll forgive,**
> **And wash all your sins away.**

"We believe the Holy Scriptures teach that the blessings of salvation are made free to all by the gospel: that it is the immediate duty of all to accept them by a cordial and obedient faith: and that nothing prevents the salvation of the greatest sinner on earth, except his own voluntary refusal to submit to the Lord Jesus Christ, which refusal will subject him to an aggravated condemnation."

How are men saved? Baptists believe it is wholly of grace. Spurgeon said, "Grace is the fountain and faith the channel through which salvation flows to the soul." Paul said, "By grace are ye saved through faith: and that not of yourselves: it is the gift of God" (Eph. 2:8). But there is no salvation except by grace through faith in Christ.

"Believe on the Lord Jesus Christ, and thou shalt be saved" (Acts 16:31). Faith in anything else will not avail. Faith in your church, your doctrines, your parents, your baptism, your confirmation, your obedience, your goodness, will not, cannot save your soul. Paul said to the Galatians, "Ye are all the children of God by faith in Christ Jesus" (Gal. 3:26).

Peter said, "Neither is there salvation in any other. For there is none other name under heaven given among men, whereby we must be saved" (Acts 4:12).

We believe this is God's plan, and hence the only plan of salvation; that God deserves all the glory, and all the redeemed will gladly sing, "Not unto us, O Lord, not unto us, but unto thy name give glory, for thy mercy, and for thy truth's sake" (Psalm 115:1). And again, "For thou wast slain, and hast redeemed us to God by the blood out of every kindred, and tongue, and people, and nation" (Rev. 5:9).

Salvation—Oh, the joyful sound,
'Tis pleasure to our ears.
A sovereign balm for every wound,
A cordial for our fears.
Buried in sorrow and in sin,
At hell's dark door we lay;
But we arise by grace divine,
To see a heavenly day.
Salvation! let the echo fly
The spacious earth around;
While all the armies of the sky
Conspire to raise the sound.

CHAPTER IV

Regeneration

"We believe that the Holy Scriptures teach that in order to be saved, we must be regenerated, or born again; that regeneration consists in giving a holy disposition to the mind, and is effected in a manner above our comprehension, by the power of the Holy Spirit, so as to secure our voluntary obedience to the gospel, and that its proper evidence is found in the holy fruits we bring forth to the glory of God."

While there is a difference, etymologically speaking, yet we use the terms *regenerated,* and *born again,* as interchangeable, meaning that operation of the Holy Spirit by which the soul is made new in Christ Jesus.

The article of faith, above quoted, says: "We must be regenerated." Without this there is no spiritual life, no communion and fellowship with the Father and with his Son Jesus Christ, no hope of eternal life resting upon God's promise and provision.

The necessity of regeneration is plainly set forth in the Saviour's words, "Except a man be born again, he cannot see the kingdom of God" (John 3:3). And again, "Verily I say unto you, Except ye be converted, and become as little children, ye shall not enter into the kingdom of heaven" (Matt. 18:3). No human act or ecclesiastical provision can possibly be a substitute for, or take the place of, this necessary act of divine power. Confession to the priest, his claim of absolution from sin, confirmation, baptism, nor aught else can serve in this connection. These are not regeneration, not the new birth, cannot be a substitute for it, neither can they produce it. They cannot unite the soul to the living head, cannot make it a child of God, an inheritor of the kingdom of Christ, and an heir of eternal life. The Saviour said, "Except ye be converted." "Except a man be born again."

How it is accomplished we know not, beyond the revealed truth. That teaches beyond question that this necessary work it wrought through the agency of the Holy Ghost. Jesus said, "It is the spirit that quickeneth" (John 6:63). The word "quicken" means to make alive. As the soul is dead, it must be made alive; hence the necessity of the Spirit's power. Paul says to Titus, "Not by works of righteousness which we have done, but according to his mercy he saved us, by the washing of regeneration, and renewing of the Holy Ghost" (Titus 3:5). Again this work is called a creation, and only God can create; not man, nor church, nor ordinance. "We are his workmanship, created in Christ Jesus unto good works" (Eph. 2:10).

Again, "Ye are washed, but ye are sanctified, but ye are justified in the name of the Lord Jesus, and by the Spirit of our God" (1 Cor. 6:11). There can be no doubt about the Agent who accomplishes this work.

Jesus said, "The wind bloweth where it listeth, and thou hearest the sound thereof, but canst not tell whence it cometh, and whither it goeth: so is every one that is born of the Spirit" (John 3:8).

I believe the above verse ought to read, "The Spirit breathes where he wills, and thou hearest his voice, but canst not tell whence it cometh nor whither it goeth; so is every one that is born of the Spirit."

Again, "Every one that loveth is born of God, and knoweth God" (1 John 4:7).

Regeneration secures our voluntary obedience to God, for we are made partakers of the divine nature. Being then new creatures, and spiritually minded, and having the spirit of Christ, "the love of Christ contraineth us." "We love him because he first loved us." Having apprehended that love and applied it to the need of our souls by faith, we joyfully seek to live well pleasing in his sight. "This is the love of God, that we keep his commandments: and his commandments are not grievous" (1 John 5:3). "If a man love me, he will keep my words" (John 14:23).

The evidence is seen in a godly walk and conversation, not loud profession of superior holiness, and claiming attainments beyond scriptural assurance. "But now being made free from sin, and become servants to God, ye have your fruit unto holiness, and the end everlasting" (Rom. 6:22).

CHAPTER V

Repentance

Baptists believe, not only in the importance, but the absolute necessity, of repentance.

The theme of John the Baptist was, "Repent ye: for the kingdom of heaven is at hand" (Matt. 3:2). Jesus preached, "Repent ye, and believe the gospel" (Mark 1:15). It is said of the apostles, "They went out, and preached that men should repent" (Mark 6:12).

Paul said to the Athenians, "The times of this ignorance God winked at; but now commandeth all men every where to repent" (Acts 17:30). Jesus settles forever the question, "Except ye repent, ye shall all likewise perish" (Luke 13:3).

Most people acknowledge the Scriptures require repentance, but many seek to substitute something more palatable to the depraved human taste than the bitterness of scriptural repentance.

What is repentance?

"The word of which it is the translation in the New Testament has as its primary meaning, afterthought, as its secondary meaning, a change of mind. It is easy to see how the secondary followed the primary signification, for in all ages after-thought has discovered reasons for a change of mind. The discovery has had a close connection with the depravity of human nature and the fallibility of human opinions. Alas, how frequent have been the occasions for a change of mind! In this change of mind, so far as scriptural repentance is concerned, a great deal is involved, as we shall see; but I wish first to show that repentance is internal. I mean by this that it is a change of the mind, the heart, and not of the life, except so far as a change of life results from a change of mind or heart."—*Dr. Pendleton's Christian Doctrine,* p. 264.

Repentance is not a form of words, is not an external act, is not reformation. Reformation is the fruit of repentance.

A repentance which does not reach the heart and affect the life will not avail for the soul. "Bring forth therefore fruits meet for repentance" (Matt. 3:8).

Paul said to the Corinthians, "Now I rejoice, not that ye were made sorry, but that ye sorrowed to repentance: for ye were made sorry after a godly manner, that ye might receive damage by us in nothing. For godly sorrow worketh repentance to salvation not to be repented of: but the sorrow of the world worketh death. For behold this selfsame thing, that ye sorrowed after a godly sort, what carefulness it wrought in you, yea, what clearing of yourselves, yea, what indignation yea, what fear, yea, what vehement desire, yea, what zeal, yea, what revenge! In all things ye have approved yourselves to be clear in this matter" (2 Cor. 7:9-11). I have given this long quotation to show that genuine repentance does produce a change in life.

Repentance involves

1. A consciousness of guilt. It is evident there could be no repentance without this. A man cannot be sorry for a guilt which he does not recognize. Man cannot be sorry for sin and turn from it unless he is conscious of being a sinner.

2. Sorrow for sin. This sorrow is not repentance, but is an essential element in repentance, "For godly sorrow worketh repentance to salvation not to be repented of." This sorrow which is "after a godly sort" (while there is no merit in it) is acceptable to God, for. "The sacrifices of God are a broken

spirit: a broken and a contrite heart, O God thou wilt not despise."

Consideration in the light of God's truth, will, by the power of the Holy Spirit, produce conviction; if the soul is honest with God and self, conviction will lead to contrition; if contrition is real, it lays the soul in submissive humility at the Saviour's feet for healing forgiveness.

3. A turning from sin. As sin dishonors God and destroys the soul, the contrite soul loathes and hates sin, and, turning from it, God delivers it from the guilt and consequences of sin. Baptists believe this to be scriptural repentance.

The afflicting of the body by tortures, self-denial of such things as God has ordained to be received with thanksgiving, keeping a man-appointed lent, or observance of such things as are called "Doing penance," cannot be a substitute in the eyes of him who said "Except ye repent, ye shall all likewise perish."

CHAPTER VI

Faith, Justification, and Santification

Baptists believe "That Repentance and Faith are sacred duties, and also inseparable graces wrought in our souls by the regenerating Spirit of God." The freeness of the blessings predicted upon these graces is set forth, "Ho, every one that thirsteth, come ye to the waters, and he that hath no money; come ye, buy, and eat; yea, come, buy wine and milk without money and without price" (Isa. 55:1).

Also in the Saviour's declaration, "Whosoever will let him take the water of life freely."

The poet expresses it—

> Ho, ye needy, come, and welcome;
> God's free bounty glorify.
> True belief and true repentance,
> Every grace that brings us nigh,
> Without money,
> Come to Jesus Christ and buy.

There is a plain and exhaustive article written by a great Christian preacher of 1,900 years ago, which will give you just what we believe on the subject of faith and justification. A sufficient extract from this article you will find by beginning at the nineteenth verse of the third chapter of Romans and reading through the fifth chapter.

"Now we know that what things soever the law saith, it saith to them who are under the law: that every mouth may be stopped, and all the world may become guilty before God.

"Therefore by the deeds of the law there shall no flesh be justified in his sight: for by the law is the knowledge of sin.

"But now the righteousness of God without the law is manifested, being witnessed by the law and the prophets;

"Even the righteousness of God which is by faith of Jesus Christ unto all and upon all them that believe: for there is no difference:

"For all have sinned, and come short of the glory of God;

"Being justified freely by his grace through the redemption that is in Christ Jesus:

"Whom God hath set forth to be a propitiation through faith in his blood, to declare his righteousness for the remission of sins that are past, through the forbearance of God;

"To declare, I say, at this time his righteousness: that he might be just, and the justifier of him which believeth in Jesus.

"Where is boasting then? It is excluded. By what law? of works? Nay: but by the law of faith.

"Therefore we conclude that a man is justified by faith without the deeds of the law.

"Is he the God of the Jews only? is he not also of the Gentiles? Yes, of the Gentiles also:

"Seeing it is one God, which shall justify the circumcision by faith, and uncircumcision through faith.

"Do we then make void the law through faith? God forbid: yea, we establish the law.

"What shall we say then that Abraham our father, as pertaining to the flesh, hath found?

"For if Abraham were justified by works, he hath whereof to glory; but not before God.

"For what saith the scripture? Abraham believed God, and it was counted unto him for righteousness.

"Now to him that worketh is the reward not reckoned of grace, but of debt.

"But to him that worketh not, but believeth on him that justifieth the ungodly, his faith is counted for righteousness.

"Even as David also describeth the blessedness of the man, unto whom God imputeth righteousness without works.

"Saying, Blessed are they whose iniquities are forgiven, and whose sins are covered.

"Blessed is the man to whom the Lord will not impute sin.

"Cometh this blessedness then upon the circumcision only, or upon the uncircumcision also? for we say that faith was reckoned to Abraham for righteousness.

"How was it then reckoned? when he was in circumcision, or in uncircumcision? Not in circumcision, but in uncircumcision.

"And he received the sign of circumcision, a seal of the righteousness of the faith which he had yet being uncircumcised: that he might be the father of all them that believe, though they be not circumcised; that righteousness might be imputed unto them also:

"And the father of circumcision to them who are not of the circumcision only; but who also walk in the steps of that faith of our father Abraham, which he had being yet uncircumcised.

"For the promise, that he should be the heir of the world, was not to Abraham, or to his seed, through the law, but through the righteousness of faith.

"For if they which are of the law be heirs, faith is made void, and the promise made of none effect:

"Because the law worketh wrath: for where no law is, there is no transgression.

"Therefore it is of faith, that it might be by grace; to the end the promise might be sure to all the seed; not to that only which is of the law, but to that also which is of the faith of Abraham; who is the father of us all,

"(As it is written, I have made thee a father of many nations,) before him whom he believed, even God, who quickeneth the dead, and calleth those things which be not as though they were.

"Who against hope believed in hope, that he might become the father of many nations, according to that which was spoken, So shall thy seed be.

"And being not weak in faith, he considered not his own body now dead, when he was about an hundred years old, neither yet the deadness of Sarah's womb:

"He staggered not at the promise of God through unbelief; but was strong in faith, giving glory to God;

"And being fully persuaded that, what he had promised, he was able also to perform.

"And therefore it was imputed to him for righteousness.

"Now it was not written for his sake alone, that it was imputed to him;

"But for us also, to whom it shall be imputed, if we believe on him that raised up Jesus our Lord from the dead;

"Who was delivered for our offences, and was raised again for our justification.

"Therefore being justified by faith, we have peace with God through our Lord Jesus Christ:

"By whom also we have access by faith into this grace wherein we stand, and rejoice in hope of the glory of God.

"And not only so, but we glory in tribulations also: knowing that tribulation worketh patience;

"And patience, experience; and experience, hope:

"And hope maketh not ashamed; because the love of God is shed abroad in our hearts by the Holy Ghost which is given unto us.

"For when we were yet without strength, in due time Christ died for the ungodly.

"For scarcely for a righteous man will one die: yet peradventure for a good man some would even dare to die.

"But God commendeth his love toward us, in that, while we were yet sinners, Christ died for us.

"Much more then, being now justified by his blood, we shall be saved from wrath through him.

"For if, when we were enemies, we were reconciled to God by the death of his Son, much more, being reconciled, we shall be saved by his life.

"And not only so, but we also joy in God through our Lord Jesus Christ, by whom we have now received the atonement.

"Wherefore, as by one man sin entered into the world, and death by sin; and so death passed upon all men, for that all have sinned:

"(For until the law sin was in the world: but sin is not imputed when there is no law.

"Nevertheless death reigned from Adam to Moses, even over them that had not sinned after the similitude of Adam's transgression, who is the figure of him that was to come.

"But not as the offence, so also is the free gift. For if through the offence of one many be dead, much more the grace of God, and the gift by grace, which is by one man, Jesus Christ, hath abounded unto many.

"And not as it was by one that sinned, so is the gift: for the judgment was by one to condemnation, but the free gift is of many offences unto justification.

"For if by one man's offence death reigned by one; much more they which receive abundance of grace and of the gift of righteousness shall reign in life by one, Jesus Christ.)

"Therefore as by the offence of one judgment came upon all men to condemnation; even so by the righteousness of one the free gift came upon all men unto justification of life.

"For as by one man's disobedience many were made sinners, so by the obedience of one shall many be made righteous.

"Moreover the law entered, that the offence might abound. But where sin abounded, grace did much more abound:

"That as sin hath reigned unto death, even so might grace reign through righteousness unto eternal life by Jesus Christ our Lord."

We believe no responsible soul can be saved without a personal faith in a personal Saviour. "He that believeth not shall be damned." "He that believeth not the Son shall not see life; but the wrath of God abideth on him."

We believe the soul is justified by faith in Christ; not by baptism, church connection, faith of parents, confirmation, the law, or any ordinance or ceremony.

"If there had been a law given which could have given life, verily righteousness should have been by the law" (Gal. 3:21). "Therefore by the works of the law shall no flesh be justified." "Therefore being justified by faith, we have peace with God through our Lord Jesus Christ: by whom also we have access by faith into this grace" (Rom. 5:1-2).

Sanctification

The primary meaning of the verb which is translated, "to sanctify," is "to hallow, to purify, to consecrate." The noun derived from this verb is defined, "consecration, sanctification."

Consecration is the "act or ceremony of separating from a common to a sacred use, or of devoting and dedicating a person or thing to the service and worship of God." As we dedicate our church buildings. We set them apart for sacred uses, the service and worship of God. As the vessels of the Temple were dedicated or sanctified for special and sacred purposes, so of God's people. "But know that the Lord hath set apart him that is godly for himself" (Psalm 4:3).

Yes, we believe too, that they are made holy by being made "partakers of the divine nature." But this righteousness is imparted, not inherent. "But of him are ye in Christ Jesus, who of God is made unto us wisdom, and righteousness, and sanctification, and redemption" (1 Cor. 1:30).

We are not sinless and perfect here in the flesh. John was not. He said, "If we say that we have no sin, we deceive ourselves, and the truth is not in us" (1 John 1:8).

Paul was not. He said, "For I know that in me (that is, in my flesh,) dwelleth no good thing: for to will is present with me; but how to perform that which is good I find not. For the good that I would I do not: but the evil which I would not, that I do" (Rom. 7:18-19).

Again he says: "But ourselves also, which have the firstfruits of the Spirit, even we ourselves groan within ourselves, waiting for the adoption, to wit, the redemption of our body" (Rom. 8:23).

That which is perfect is in the future. "But when that which is perfect is come, then that which is in part shall be done away" (1 Cor. 13:10).

CHAPTER VII

Perseverance or Preservation

"We believe that the Holy Scriptures teach that such only are real believers as endure unto the end; that their persevering attachment to Christ is the grand mark which distinguishes them from superficial professors; that a special Providence watches over their welfare; and they are kept by the power of God through faith unto salvation."

Yes, Baptists believe that such as are real believers, "Being rooted and grounded in love," "Rooted and built up in him and established in the faith," shall endure to the end. We think the Scriptures aboundantly prove this doctrine.

Unless this is true we have no definition of the word "save." Its primary meaning is to make safe, and all of its definitions comport with this idea.

Now, if a soul is saved, it is made safe by the divine, infinite power of God. We might rest the case here, but as the proof of this doctrine is so ample, we are not content to pass it over thus, lest someone fail to see the truth.

"He that believeth on the Son hath everlasting life" (John 3:36). "He that heareth my word, and believeth on him that sent me, hath everlasting life" (John 5:24).

The Scriptures declare positively that a personal faith in Jesus secures to the believer the gift of everlasting life. Now, I simply ask the question, How long will it be till that life ends? Until it does end the believing, trusting soul will not be subject to the penalty of eternal death.

The word here translated "everlasting" is used in forty-three places in the New Testament to qualify life, or fix the duration of the believer's life. It is the same word the Saviour used to describe the duration of the punishment of the wicked and the happiness of the saved. (Matthew 25:46.) It is the same word used in Romans 16:26 to describe the character of God's existence. The same used in 2 Timothy 2:10 to describe the duration of the glory of Christ: in 2 Peter 1:11 to describe the duration of Christ's kingdom.

Then just so long as God is, so long as the kingdom and glory of Christ endure, so long is the true believer safe. So long will his spiritual life and happiness endure.

Will someone say, "It is a dangerous doctrine to teach"? Well, I reply, I had rather risk the judgment of Christ on that matter than yours or mine. It is the doctrine Christ taught. It is simply our business to teach the Word. God will take care of the results.

Again, our case is clearly made out, but as if to make assurance doubly sure, Jesus says: "I give unto them eternal life; and they shall never perish, and no one shall snatch them out of my hand. My Father, who hath given them unto me, is greater than all; and no one is able to snatch them out of my Father's hand" (John 10:28-29, ASV).

I like the term "preservation" better than "perseverance." The former indicates the power by which we are kept, the latter the result of that keeping. "Kept by the power of God through faith unto salvation" (1 Peter 1:15).

Two children talking, one said: "How is it we are not lost and left and forgotten as we go on through this life?" The other answered: "God reaches down his hand, we take hold on his hand, and he leads us all the way through life." "But," said the first, "we go to sleep and could not hold on to God's hand." The answer came: "I got that wrong. God takes hold of our hand and he does not go to sleep." "Kept by the power of God."

CHAPTER VIII

The Church

Baptists believe that a church of Jesus Christ is a body of baptized believers, associated together in one place to preach the gospel, to keep the ordinances and represent the interests of Christ's kingdom in the world.

Baptists are not simply set for a defense of the truth, "to earnestly contend for the faith which was once delivered to the saints," to carry out the injunctions of the Holy Spirit given us through Paul, "Keep the ordinances as I delivered them unto you," to require in all the evidences of regeneration and conversion, but also to see that the spiritual house is builded and governed according to the divine directions. "See, saith he, that thou make all things according to the pattern showed to thee in the mount." With Baptists it is not a question of taste, or convenience, or popularity, but, what are the divine directions and pattern? "Christ is the head of the church," the "one Lawgiver in Zion," and no man nor set of men can rightfully change what he has established and fixed.

There was no such organization as the church of Christ until Christ builded it.

He said, "Upon this rock I will build my church." It was, then, at the time of speaking, in the future. Those who claim the Jewish nation was a church must acknowledge that it was a corrupt church, and crucified the Lord. Where Stephen speaks of the church in the wilderness, Acts 7:38, the translation should be congregation. Everyone knows there was no such organization at that time as the church Christ builded in the world.

In the New Testament, where only we can find in the Scriptures any reference to the church of Christ, some think the word is used sometimes to denote all the saints, or all the saved, as, "Christ is the head of the church." "Christ also loved the church, and gave himself for it" (Eph. 5:25). "The general assembly and church of the firstborn, which are written in heaven" (Heb. 12:23). This last will evidently be local when they shall have assembled.

The word translated "church" originally meant "called out," and was used to denote any secular, local assembly, as in Acts 19:32-41. So in the highest and holiest sense all the redeemed are called out, and it is fitly applied to them.

The word used in the New Testament usually refers to a local assembly or congregation of the followers of Christ associated and covenanted together, for religious worship and work. These are the only kind of New Testament churches on earth. They are local, independent bodies, subject to no central power; governed by the New Testament code, and amenable only to Christ the living head. This is clearly evident from such expressions as: "The church which was at Jerusalem," "and when they had ordained them elders in every church," "gathered the church together," "the church in their house," "the church that was at Antioch," "the church of Ephesus," "the church in Smyrna," "in Perganos," etc.

Again! "The churches of Galatia," "the churches of Asia," "the churches of Macedonia," "the churches of Judaea," "the seven churches which are in Asia," etc.

The New Testament knows nothing of a church covering a given extent of territory, such as the "Church of England," "The Protestant Episcopal Church of America," "The Church of Scotland," etc. It knows nothing of an aggregate of a denomination called by the name of church, as the "Presbyterian Church," "The Methodist Episcopal Church," "The Roman Catholic Church," etc. In the days of the apostles, they had churches, but nothing visible and tangible organized in any shape and known as the church, except local congregations, as clearly seen from the above Scriptures.

The term "church" is never applied in the Scriptures to any aggregate of churches, either territorially or ecclesiastically.

Baptists, following the New Testament pattern, have no

aggregate known as "The Baptist Church." Like the apostles and early Christians we have churches.

Even history clearly proves this position. "The churches in those early times were entirely independent, none of them subject to any foreign jurisdiction, but each one governed by its own rulers and its own laws" (Mosheim, vol. 1, cent. 1, chap. 14, p. 107).

"The societies, which were instituted in the cities of the Roman Empire, were united only by the ties of faith and charity. Independence and equality formed the basis of their internal constitution" (Gibbon, "Decline and Fall," vol. 1, p. 554).

"Though there was one Lord, one faith, one baptism for all of them, yet they were each a distinct, independent community . . . not having any recognized head on earth, or acknowledging any sovereignty of one of these societies over others" (Archbishop Whately, Km. of Christ, p. 36). How is that for an admission of one of the greatest of the men whose church lays exclusive claim to apostolic succession?

Errors in the formation and government of churches lead to errors in doctrine and practice. Baptists believe the New Testament plan to be good enough, and hence we cling to the scriptural form and government. Jesus commanded (Matt. 18:17) to tell a certain kind of grievance to the church, after other divinely given measures had failed.

Imagine an Episcopalian, a Methodist, Presbyterian, or Catholic attempting to obey the injunction, and telling his grievance to his church.

CHAPTER IX

Church Members and Officers

Baptists believe that only regenerated, converted people ought to become members of the church.

They believe the only scripturally authorized officers of a church are pastors and deacons. Why?

The whole tenor of Scripture teaching confirms the principle of regeneration, conversion preceding church membership. Otherwise there could be no separation between the world and the church. In any country where the principles of any church which ignores this fundamental scriptural doctrine prevail, just to that extent is obliterated the lines which distinguish Christians from the world.

If the probationary system, or infant baptism and infant membership were universal, as its advocates desire, then in one generation all the unregenerated people would be in the churches.

The safe, right, scriptural, God-given principle is: "First gave their own selves to the Lord, and unto us by the will of God" (2 Cor. 8:5).

The profession which is made, the work to be done, the duties and obligations assumed, all necessarily presuppose a radical internal change of the one becoming a member of a church of Jesus Christ.

The Scriptures clearly and unmistakably bear out this condition of things. The members of the churches are professedly the friends of Jesus and children of God.

Jesus said: "Ye are my friends if ye do whatsoever I command you." "If ye were of the world, the world would love his own." "Ye must be born again."

"Except ye be converted, and become as little children, ye shall not enter into the kingdom of heaven" (Matt. 18:3).

The Word describes God's children as being "dead unto sin but alive unto God through Jesus Christ our Lord," "spiritually minded," having "the Spirit of Christ," "risen with Christ."

The churches of Christ are not reformatory schools, are not organizations into which natural men are to be taken and by the process of law, ceremony, or ordinance made children of God, but each ought to be a congregation of God's people, separated from the world.

No unconverted man or woman can meet the duties and obligations of a church member, and should not assume such responsibilities.

This is a doctrine peculiarly and distinctively Baptistic, entirely scriptural and consistent. We can't see their motives and read their hearts. They may be deceived and may deceive us, but they must claim to be regenerated before they can obtain membership in a Baptist church.

It was so in the days of the apostles. "They that gladly received his word were baptized." "And the Lord added unto them day by day those that were saved" (ASV).

Again, members of Baptist churches become such by their own voluntary act.

You can no more make a Baptist by force or coercion than you could make a man a Mason who did not wish it.

Baptist churches ought to be entirely composed of "a people made willing in the day of his power." Not by birth, inherent goodness, ritual or ordinance. To them that believe on his name he gives power to become the children of God. Belief is a personal, voluntary matter. It is the result of the Holy Spirit's teaching and power, and brings liberty—makes free.

The bond of union is fellowship, and this cannot be forced. Its essence is confidence and love, and these must be free and voluntary.

This doctrine is distinctively Baptist. No parent, preacher, or earthly power can force anyone against his will to this step, and if such attempt were made any true Baptist church would resent it.

Roman Catholics have through all the past opposed and denounced this freedom of conscience. They have fought it with every means at their command. The prison and the stake have ever been their argument against it where they dared to use them.

Every state church has in a greater or less degree shown this intolerance to soul liberty.

Officers

The Scriptures know nothing of a graded ministry.

The word "bishop" means an overseer. It meant simply a pastor of a church. Every pastor of a scriptural church is a New Testament bishop. The titles of elder and bishop are applied to the same individual. Paul sent from Miletus "to Ephesus, and called the elders of the church." Addressing these same elders, he says, "Take heed therefore unto yourselves, and to all the flock, over which the Holy Ghost hath made you overseers." Paul writes "to all the saints in Christ Jesus which are at Philippi, with the bishops and deacons."

Episcopalian scholars acknowledge that in New Testament times elder and bishop were the same, and therefore no such order obtained as diocesan episcopacy.

"It is a fact now generally recognized by theologians of all shades of opinion, that in the language of the New Testament the same officer in the church is called indifferently bishop and elder or presbyter."—(Bishop Lightfoot, *Commentary on Philippians,* p. 95.)

As to ruling elders. There is this single passage: "Let the elders that rule well be counted worthy of double honour, especially they who labour in the word and doctrine" (1 Tim. 5:17).

Look at it, and parse it, and if then you can find in it a foundation on which to build a distinct and separate class of church officers, it is of no use to argue with you on the subject. If anyone believes it, it must be because he wishes to, and not because of evidence.

CHAPTER X

Baptism—What Is It?

Baptists believe that baptism is the dipping, immersion in water, in the name of the Trinity, of a believer upon profession of faith, by one duly authorized by a church of Jesus Christ to perform such service.

All denominations admit this to be scriptural baptism, yet many claim it is not the only baptism. Others claim the act may be pouring or sprinkling water upon the person. Many, that unconscious, irresponsible infants are proper subjects to receive baptism; some even claim that it is necessary to salvation.

There is no doubt about the immersion of a believer being scriptural baptism. All admit it. All denominations accept it as such. There is of necessity great doubt about anything else being baptism. Then why be in doubt when you can be sure you are right? Baptists never doubt the scripturalness of their baptism.

Besides, Paul says, "One Lord, one faith, one baptism, one God and Father of all," etc. Now if you believe Paul, or the Holy Spirit, when he says "one Lord, one faith, one God," why doubt his word or contradict him when he says "*one* baptism? If immersion is baptism, then sprinkling and pouring are not baptism. Only one is, can be, right.

The word *baptidzo* is not a translation of the word used in the original, but only transferred, only one or two letters in the Greek being changed.

I could give you the names of more than forty Greek lexicons, all of which give as the primary meaning of the word to dip, to immerse, and no standard lexicon gives any definition to the word which is really at variance with this accepted meaning. None of them give sprinkle or pour as a meaning of the word.

Besides, if you substitute sprinkle or pour in any of the passages and attempt to read it, you will find it will not fit. Take Mark 1:5, "And were all sprinkled of him in the river of Jordon"; or "were all *poured* of him in the river of Jordan." But it is correct to say: "Were all *immersed* or *dipped* of him in the river of Jordan."

Affusionists sprinkle the water, not the people; so if sprinkling is baptism, then it is water, and not the people, baptized.

In all Greek literature the word *baptidzo* means to dip, plunge, immerse. Dr. Conant has collected about seventy-five passages from profane Greek literature in which the word occurs, and in every instance the meaning is plainly the same as in the Scriptures, namely, immerse.

The Greek is a very precise language, having a word for every shade of meaning, so much so that often nice shades of meaning in Greek cannot be clearly expressed in English. In Greek there is a distinct word for sprinkle, but it is never used in a single passage where baptism is mentioned. The same is true of the word for pour.

The Greek language has, like all others, undergone many changes, but the Greeks today, knowing the meaning of their own language, adhere strictly to immersion for baptism. Even the Presbyterian missionaries in Athens today are compelled to practice immersion even upon infants, as the Greek church has always done. *Baptidzo* means to dip just as much as the English word "dip" does.

Leading scholars of all denominations have frankly acknowledged that the scriptural and apostolic baptism was immersion. Dean Stanley, one of the most prominent of the Episcopal clergy of England, said: "For the first thirteen centuries the almost universal practice of baptism was that of which we read in the New Testament, and which is the very meaning of the word "baptize," that those who were baptized were plunged, submerged, immersed into the water. The change from immersion to sprinkling has set aside the larger part of the apostolic language regarding baptism, and has altered the very meaning of the word." He frankly acknowledges that in the days of Christ and the apostles, the word did not mean to sprinkle, but to immerse.

John Calvin, the founder of the Presbyterian church, in its present form, said: "The very word baptize, itself, signifies to immerse; and it is certain that immersion was observed by the ancient church." Commenting on the baptism of the eunuch, he says: "Here we perceive how baptism was administered among the ancients, for they immersed the whole body in water."

John Wesley, founder of Methodism, on Romans 6:4, says, "We are buried with him, alluding to the ancient manner of baptizing by immersion."

Martin Luther says: "For to baptize in Greek is to dip, and baptizing is dipping. Being moved by this reason, I would have those who are to be baptized to be altogether dipped into the water, as the word doth express, and as the mystery doth signify."—(Works. Wittemb. Ed., vol. 2, p. 79.)

Cardinal Gibbons, Roman Catholic, says: "For several centuries after the establishment of Christianity, baptism was usually conferred by immersion, but since the twelfth century the practice of baptizing by affusion has prevailed in the Catholic Church, as this manner is attended with less inconvenience than baptism by immersion."—*Faith of Our Fathers*, p. 275.

The *Encyclopaedia Brittanica*, in the article "Baptism," vol. 3, p. 351, says: "The usual mode of performing the ceremony was by immersion. . . . The council of Ravenna, in 1311, was the first council of the church to legalize sprinkling by leaving it to the choice of the officiating minister." We could multiply such testimony from those who practice sprinkling, but space forbids. If any honestly believe that Christ did ordain sprinkling for baptism (though certainly in that case it would never have been called baptism), I can respect them for following their convictions, but when they admit Jesus was immersed, and commanded his followers to follow his example, and yet say, I prefer to do something else, it looks to me like wilful disobedience.

In our next chapter we will show from the Scriptures the proof of our position.

CHAPTER XI

Baptism—Immersion

A cultured lady, reared a Catholic, made profession of faith in Christ. The Episcopalians, Methodists, and Presbyterians were soliciting her to join their respective churches. I was a visitor at the home prior to her profession of conversion. When I called after this event, I said: "I am not going to run after you to get you to join my church, but I have one request to make of you." She asked, "What is the request?" I replied, "Before you join any church carefully and prayerfully read the New Testament with a view of learning your duty, and then do whatever it requires." She answered, "I will do that." She did, and as a result joined a Baptist church. One of her former solicitors said: "Well, I suppose you have done right to join the Baptists, even if you did have to sacrifice principle to go with them."

She resented the imputation, and said frankly: "I have made no sacrifice of principle. I joined a Baptist church after careful and prayerful investigation, because I believe them to teach and hold the doctrine and ordinances as taught by Christ and the apostles, fully persuaded I was following the Divine teaching."

Here is some of the evidence she had from the Scriptures on baptism:

"Then went out to him Jerusalem, and all Judaea, and all the region round about Jordan, and were baptized of him in Jordan, confessing their sins" (Matt. 3:5-6).

Now, if I should say, any number of converts joined the First Baptist Church in Eufaula, and on a certain day I baptized them all in the Chattahoochee river, no one would have any trouble to understand what was done or how the baptizing was performed. Yet Matthew's statement is equally as plain.

Affusionists do not sprinkle and pour their candidates while in the river.

"And Jesus, when he was baptized, went up straightway out of the water" (Matt. 3:16).

Did anyone ever see anything like that at a sprinkling or pouring? Do the babies or adults go up out of the water after they are sprinkled?

"And there went out unto him all the land of Judaea, and they of Jerusalem, and were all baptized of him in the river of Jordan, confessing their sins" (Mark 1:5).

Here the statement is plain and positive, "in the river of Jordan." Literally "in the Jordan river."

"And it came to pass in those days, that Jesus came from Nazareth of Galilee, and was baptized of John in Jordan. And straightway coming up out of the water, he saw the heavens opened, and the Spirit like a dove descending upon him" (Mark 1:9-10).

Now, candidly, it must take a great deal of imagination to see anything but an immersion in that plain, simple statement. No one would ever suspect anything else unless prejudicial training supplanted the plain teaching of the Word. A great many people are thoroughly convinced that Jesus was immersed in the Jordan, but vainly excuse themselves from following the Master's example.

A message came to me that a lady wished to talk to me on the subject of baptism. I called at her house. Before I entered the door she began to parade her objections against immersion. I said: "Madam, if you were thoroughly convinced that Jesus was immersed, would you be immersed?" Her reply was: "No, I would not." I simply said, "Good evening," and walked away without entering the house.

I was on the train with a good Methodist brother. He introduced the subject of baptism. I said: "Do you believe that Jesus was immersed?" He answered: "If he was, it does not follow that I should be immersed." I pressed the question, asking him to say yes or no. After a number of evasions and attempted explanations, he finally answered: "Yes, I believe he was immersed in the river." Now, if baptism could mean a dozen things, which it does not, and cannot, still I would never be satisfied to be baptized in any way different from the example the Saviour set us. Many others are not satisfied, but still refuse to obey.

No one has ever been able to explain away the plain facts set forth in the baptism of the eunuch, which facts are about as clear a claim for immersion as words could present.

"And they went down both into the water, both Philip and the eunuch; and he baptized him. And when they were come up out of the water, the Spirit of the Lord caught away Philip, that the eunuch saw him no more: and he went on his way rejoicing" (Acts 8:38-39). Now, some have tried to quibble about the Greek preposition *apo* (used in the account of the Saviour's baptism, and translated "out of") not meaning *out of,* but *from.* Here in this case *apo* is not used, but *ek,* and its literal primary meaning is out of. Affusionists have attempted to make capital out of the expression used concerning Paul's baptism, "Arise, and be baptized," saying that "he arose, stood up, and was baptized," the very thing he must have done if immersed, and the very thing he would not have done if sprinkled.

Paul certainly ought to have been a competent witness of how it was done; and here is what he says about it: "Therefore we are buried with him by baptism into death: that like as Christ was raised up from the dead by the glory of the Father, even so we also should walk in newness of life. For if we have been planted together in the likeness of his death, we shall be also in the likeness of his resurrection" (Rom. 6:4-5).

"Buried with him in baptism, wherein also ye are risen with him through the faith of the operation of God, who hath raised him from the dead" (Col. 2:12).

Certainly, if a burial and resurrection are to be represented in baptism—and there is no room for doubt unless Paul was mistaken—then only a dipping, an immersion, can possibly fill the conditions required.

In none of the New Testament baptisms is the act of immersion in anywise impracticable or improbable. Many of the accounts and references to the ordinance demand an immersion to fill the conditions plainly set forth. Baptists believe immersion alone is baptism, because Christ was immersed in the river. John baptized in the river. The apostles practiced immersion, for Paul calls it a burial and resurrection. Both Philip and the eunuch went down into the water, and after Philip had baptized him they came up out of the water. Many others believe with us but prefer to follow Rome rather than to obey Christ.

CHAPTER XII

Washings in the New Testament

Since pedobaptists have tried so hard to make capital out of the New Testament *washings,* that is, the translation of the word *baptidzo* by wash, we have decided to devote this article to an explanation of these washings. In Mark 7:3, "For the Pharisees, and all the Jews, except they wash their hands oft, eat not," the word is not *baptidzo,* but *nipto* (here the third person plural *nipsontai*). It is never used to denote the ordinance of baptism or an immersion, but the washing of parts, as the hands, the feet, the eyes. The word is never translated baptize in any instance. It does not mean the same thing as wash in the fourth verse: "And when they come from the market except they wash [*baptidzontai*], they eat not." Dr. Eaton, *Faith of Baptists,* p. 27, says, "Mark, writing primarily for the Romans, stops to explain the absurd lengths to which the Pharisees carried their cleanings."

"For the Pharisees, and all the Jews, except they wash [*nipsontai*] their hands oft [the Greek is, with the fist], eat not, holding the tradition of the elders. And when they come from the market, except they wash [*baptidzontai*], they eat not. And many other things there be, which they have received to hold, as the washing [*baptismous*] of cups, and pots, brasen vessels." Now there would have been no point in Mark's stopping to explain that the Pharisees went to the great length of sprinkling or pouring water upon themselves on returning from market, when they, while at home, washed diligently or "with the fist" before eating. That they would go to the lenth of immersing themselves on returning from market, where Gentiles had touched them, was a remarkable thing, and worth explaining to the Romans, who did not know the customs of the Pharisees and strict Jews. Meyer, in loco, says: "In this case *ean ma baptidzontai* is not to be understood of washing the hands, but of immersion, which the word in classic Greek and in the

New Testament everywhere denotes, *i. e.,* in this case, according to context, to take a bath. Having come from market where they may have contracted pollution through contact with the crowd, they eat not without having first bathed.

"As for the immersion of cups and pots and brasen vessels; that was simply carrying out the ceremonial law, given in Leviticus 11:32: 'And upon whatsoever any of them, when they are dead, doth fall, it shall be unclean; whether it be any vessel of wood, or raiment, or skin, or sack, whatsoever vessel it be, wherein any work is done, it must be put into water, and it shall be unclean until the even; so it shall be cleansed.'

"The cups and pots were of wood, and these with the brasen vessels were to be immersed for cleansing, when they became ceremonially unclean, while earthen vessels were to be broken. The word rendered 'tables' in the common version *klion* does not belong to the true text, and the revisers very properly omitted it.

"It is an interesting and significant fact that in after years, copyists, not understanding the customs of the Pharisees, came to this passage, and thought the word *baptidzo* must be a mistake, since it seemed out of the question that Pharisees should actually immerse themselves when they came from market. So the copyists ventured to strike out *baptidzo* and insert *rantidzo,* which means to sprinkle. They never suspected that *baptidzo* could mean sprinkle, or pour, or they would not have made the substitution."

"And when they come from the market, except they wash, they eat not. And many other things there be, which they have received to hold, as the washing of cups, and pots, brasen vessels, and of tables" (Mark 7:4).

"For laying aside the commandment of God, ye hold the tradition of men, as the washing of pots and cups: and many other such like things ye do" (Mark 7:8).

"And when the Pharisee saw it, he marvelled that he had not first washed before dinner" (Luke 11:38). "Which stood only in meats and drinks, and divers washings, and carnal ordinances, imposed on them until the time of reformation" (Heb. 9:10).

In the above passages the translation of *baptidzo* is wash, and only in these. Some have hooted at the idea of a Jew who had been to the market dipping himself before eating, but that was exactly what he did, and what Jewish tradition required him to do.

Maimonides, the great Jewish writer, of whom the encyclopedia says: His importance for the religion and science of Judaism, and his influence upon their development is so gigantic that he has rightly been placed second to Moses, the great law-giver himself, says: "If they had been to market and mingled with persons ceremonially unclean they were defiled and in a laver that holds forty seahs (about sixty gallons) of water every defiled man dips himself. And so when a Jew came from the market he dipped himself in water before he would eat."

So the Pharisees marveled (were greatly surprised) that Jesus did not perform this ablution, dip himself before eating.

But this was not God's law, or requirement, but only a Jewish tradition, and was not binding on him who came to break down the middle wall, or partition, between Jew and Gentile. There were certain washings, dippings, bathings which God did require, as in Leviticus 15:1-13. Jesus never disobeyed any command of God, but often showed contempt for the traditions which men had substituted for God's requirements, and by which they made the commands of God of no effect. "But he answered and said unto them, Why do ye also transgress the commandment of God by your tradition? . . . But in vain they do worship me, teaching for doctrines the commandments of men" (Matt. 15:3-9).

CHAPTER XIII

Believers' Baptism

Baptists believe that only penitent believers are scriptural subjects for baptism. Only such as have repented of sin, believed to the saving of the soul, been saved by divine power, regenerated by the Holy Spirit, created anew in Christ Jesus, converted to God, are prepared to receive the ordinance. We think the design of baptism, the act, the symbolic representation, all require the subject to be a child of God, dead to sin and alive unto God through faith in the Lord Jesus Christ.

To administer baptism to anyone, whether infant or adult, that has not repented, believed, and been converted, is to misplace the ordinance and make a misrepresentation to the world. Pedobaptists say, "It is an outward sign of an inward grace." Then if the inward grace does not exist, they make a misrepresentation. If, as some of them say, it is a symbol of the regeneration or purification (as they are so fond of calling baptism), they publish a falsehood to the world whenever they baptize anyone who does not profess to have a heart purified by faith.

The duty to be baptized rests solely upon the authoritative command of Christ. As no act can be scriptural baptism except that which Christ authorized, so no one can be a scriptural subject except such as the command embraces. The Commission given by the divine Master is, "Go ye therefore, and teach all nations, baptizing them" (Matt. 28:19).

Now all scholars and commentators agree that the word "teach" in this verse means to disciple, or make disciples.

Paul, in Romans 6:4, and Colossians 2:12, calls baptism a burial, and clearly teaches that it is also a resurrection. We bury only the dead, and none but the dead are to be raised from the dead. Only those dead to sin are to be buried with Christ in baptism, and those alive unto God arise to walk in newness of life.

The Scriptures are addressed to responsible, intelligent beings.

The gospel makes no requirements of the irresponsible—infants and idiots. We gladly believe that God has graciously provided for these, but he has laid no commands upon them.

The command to baptize believers precludes the right of baptism to all who are not believers. The specified qualifications for baptism exclude all from the ordinance who have not met these qualifications.

If a man should instruct his agent to buy for him any number of trained horses, that would not authorize the agent to purchase colts or other stock. The instruction to buy *trained* horses would preclude the right to buy any but trained horses. So the Master's command to baptize believers forbids the baptizing of any who are not believers.

So much for the Commission. Now let us see how the apostles and inspired writers understood and carried out this Commission. The first account of baptism, after the

Great Commission given by the risen Lord, is found in Acts 2:41-44: "Then they that gladly received his word were baptized: and the same day there were added unto them about three thousand souls. And they continued steadfastly in the apostles' doctrine and fellowship, and in breaking of bread, and in prayers. And fear came upon every soul: and many wonders and signs were done by the apostles. And all that believed were together, and had all things common." That was certainly believers' baptism. They "gladly received his word." "And all that believed were together."

Acts 5:14: "And believers were the more added unto the Lord, multitudes both of men and women."

The text does not say they were baptized, yet no one doubts it. They were believers, men and women.

Acts 8:12: "But when they believed Philip preaching the things concerning the kingdom of God, and the name of Jesus Christ, they were baptized, both men and women."

Notice those baptized were men and women—no infants, and they were believing men and women. Whatever may be said of the spuriousness of Acts 8:37, yet there is undoubted evidence of the eunuch believing before Philip baptized him.

Saul was praying and God heard him before Ananias went to him. He certainly was a believer prior to his baptism. "Can any man forbid water, that these should not be baptized, which have received the Holy Ghost as well as we" (Acts 10:47)? They heard the Word, while Peter was preaching the Holy Spirit was given. They spake with tongues and magnified the Lord.

Of Lydia it is said, "Whose heart the Lord opened, that she attended unto the things which were spoken of Paul. And when she was baptized, and her household" (Acts 16:14-15). Now, in verse 40, we read of this household, "And when they had seen the brethren, they comforted them, and departed."

Of the jailer at Philippi, we read in Acts 16:32, "And they spake unto him the word of the Lord, and to all that were in his house." Then they were all subjects of gospel address, capable of receiving the message of life from Paul and Silas. Verses 33 and 34 read: "And he took them the same hour of the night, and washed their stripes; and was baptized, he and all his, straightway. And when he had brought them into his house, he set meat before them, and rejoiced, believing in God with all his house." Now, they heard the Word, they believed, they rejoiced, they were baptized. So Baptists believe and practice.

"And Crispus, the chief ruler of the synagogue, believed on the Lord with all his house; and many of the Corinthians hearing believed, and were baptized" (Acts 18:8).

So Crispus and the Corinthians were baptized believers. There is not a single instance of infant baptism in the New Testament, not even an inference that has any scriptural support. There is not the slightest evidence that anyone received the ordinance of baptism who did not profess faith in Christ; hence Baptists have ever held to believers' baptism.

CHAPTER XIV

Design of Baptism

Baptists believe that scriptural baptism is a "setting forth of the believer's death to sin, burial to the world, entrance through a new birth into a new life, faith in the burial and resurrection of Christ and by consequence of his own resurrection, and if baptism symbolizes purification, then the subjection of his whole being to the purifying and sanctifying influences of the Holy Spirit." (Burrows, *Symbols of Baptism.*)

Baptists have often been accused of making too much of baptism, simply because they practice what they believe, and they believe with Paul, that there is "one Lord, one faith, one baptism."

No one believes that Jesus was baptized three or four different ways, but *one* way. That one way is baptism, and all other ways are not baptism. Most people who have investigated the subject believe that Jesus was immersed in the river Jordan. Baptists believe this, and because they have the courage of their convictions, and practice what they believe, they are styled illiberal, close, narrow, selfish, and bigoted, and accused of making too much of baptism. Don't be alarmed, brethren; they said worse things than that about our Master. "Stand fast." "Endure hardness as a good soldier of Jesus Christ." Baptists believe that no one is a scriptural subject for baptism till he is already saved. All well-informed people know that we teach this: then upon what ground can they say we believe baptism essential to salvation?

We believe it is a positive command, enjoined upon the believing, saved soul, and is essential to true, loving obedience. And we believe if such believers were properly informed and not prejudiced against the truth, they would all want to obey the Saviour in this simple yet sublime ordinance.

Baptists are the only denomination who are not amenable to the charge of making too much of baptism. The Catholics and some other pedobaptists attach a meaning and an importance to baptism not authorized by Scripture. In each and all there is a tinge of the doctrine of baptismal regeneration. But for this, infant baptism would never have been invented. The doctrines of the Catholics, Episcopalians, and Campbellites avow their belief in the necessity of baptism in order to be saved. Very many pedobaptists also believe in baptismal regeneration, not because the Scriptures teach it, but because of the emphasis placed upon it by their books and teachers. If not, why rush off in such frantic haste to have a dying baby sprinkled? Such an act cannot confer any earthly good or privilege, for it is just ready to leave all that is earthly.

Baptists believe that the immersion of a believer is an open declaration to the world that such a one is dead to sin. "Likewise reckon ye also yourselves to be dead indeed unto sin, but alive unto God through Jesus Christ our Lord" (Rom. 6:11). And because he is dead to the world and to sin, he is to be buried, and in a spiritual sense is separated from these. Again, the immersion is a proclamation to the world that we believe in him who "died for our sins according to the scriptures; and that he was buried, and that he rose again the third day according to the scriptures." So it is a proclamation of our belief that Christ arose from the dead, and in this symbol and object lesson is set forth this resurrection of Christ to the world. Likewise it symbolizes not only our rising to walk in newness of life here, but proclaims the resurrection of our bodies, when they that are in their graves shall hear the voice of the Son of God, and they that have done good shall come forth unto the resurrection of life eternal.

As we believe that baptism so appropriately teaches these great fundamental truths, and so beautifully symbolizes so much of Christ's work, the believer's experience, the Christian's hopes, the promises of God, and the provisions of the gospel, is it strange that we contend for that one act which is baptism, that qualification which entitles one to baptism, and strict obedience to the command of the great Captain of our salvation, and conformity to the example he set for us when he was baptized of John in Jordan? Baptism scripturally understood and properly administered preaches to the world the great underlying principles, the fundamental doctrine of the glorious gospel of Christ. In this simple but sublime object lesson we have a beautiful, impressive sermon which says to all beholders, We were dead in sins, helpless, hopeless, and lost. The great Saviour of sinners had compassion on us, he took our place, died in our stead, died that we might live. He arose again from the dead according to his promise, and according to the prophecy and Word of God. Then through the power of God's truth and the Holy Spirit we died to sin, and being made alive unto God through Jesus Christ our Lord, we arise to walk in newness of life. We also declare by this simple and divinely appointed ordinance our hope in the resurrection of our bodies from the grave, when the fullness of the time for the redemption of our bodies shall come. Then, these vile bodies shall be changed and fashioned like unto the glorified body of our Lord Jesus Christ, when the time comes for the full satisfaction of God's children and they shall awake in his likeness.

CHAPTER XV

The Proper Administrator of Baptism

In chapter X, the statement is made: "Baptists believe that baptism is the dipping, immersion in water, in the name of the Trinity, of a believer upon profession of faith, by one duly authorized by a church of Jesus Christ to perform such service."

Bear in mind they believe that scriptural baptism is only properly, scripturally administered by one duly authorized by a church of Jesus Christ.

The Scriptures require a certain act—immersion; and a proper subject—a penitent, believing person professing faith in Christ. It is appropriate for the ordinance to be administered by one duly authorized by a local church.

An improper act or an improper candidate renders the baptism improper, unscriptural, and invalid.

Christ is the head of the church, the one law-giver in Zion. The churches are the executors of his will and law. Christ gave the law and obeyed it, established the ordinances and kept them; he set us an example, saying, "Follow me."

Baptists are charged with being sticklers for forms. Yes, but the form for which we contend is a divine form, ordained by God, observed by Christ, and enjoined upon his followers. To his churches he has committed the ordinances. These ordinances (baptism and the Lord's Supper) are holy symbols of God's own appointment, setting forth in object lessons the fundamental principles and doctrine of the gospel of salvation through Christ Jesus. Now if God punished his people, blotted out Israel, scattering them among the nations, because they kept not his ordinances and refused to walk in his statutes, who shall dare to change and trifle with these simple, sublime ordinances, which reflect the glory of Christ's work, life, death, burial, and resurrection? The condition of God's blessings upon ancient Israel was: "That ye keep mine ordinances." And under his dire punishment he stoops to explain, saying: "Ye have gone away from mine ordinances and have not kept them," and even compassionately to invite them, saying, "Return unto me and I will return unto you." Surely God in his holiness, justice, and consistency is not less concerned about these ordinances, which set before men the finished work of Christ, than the temporary ordinances which shadowed forth his coming.

But who shall administer them? If they are church ordinances, then they are necessarily under the control of the churches, and only such as the churches appoint (ordain) are qualified for this service.

Baptists believe that since in its introduction baptism was administered by divine authority, and since there is no declaration of a change in the method of administering the ordinance, there should be a commission from God to administer the ordinance now. John said he was sent to baptize with water (John 1:33). True, there has been no direct personal command to the preachers of this day from God, but Jesus commands his church, in Matthew 28:19, to teach (make disciples) all nations, baptizing them, etc. It is, of course, not expected that a church as an organization does the baptizing, but that it is done by the order of and under the direction of the church; and hence one is thus authorized to baptize by the church and for the church, which has a commission from Jesus to *go,* to *teach,* to *baptize.* As Jesus made and baptized more disciples than John (though Jesus himself baptized not, but his disciples—John 4:1-2), so a church in obedience to the Commission (Matt. 28:19) makes and baptizes disciples, though the church baptizes not, but her selected and duly appointed ministry. If the Commission to evangelize the world is to the church, then the command to baptize is to the church, and hence baptism administered by the authority of a scriptural church is by divine commandment as truly as was that of John the Baptist. . . . Since the command is to the church, it is appropriate that the administrator of baptism be under the direction of and authorized by a scriptural church.

Surely Jesus intended to emphasize the importance of scriptural baptism when he "came from Nazareth of Galilee, and was baptized of John in Jordan."

CHAPTER XVI

The Lord's Supper

Jesus appointed two simple ordinances in his church to be observed till the end of time. As baptism is a symbol of his burial and resurrection, so the Lord's Supper is commemorative of his death and sufferings. Both set forth in beautiful symbol great fundamental doctrines of the gospel. Each was appointed, authorized, established, fixed by himself. They belong only to his churches.

Neither churches nor individuals have any right to change the form, the order, or design of these simple, yet sublime, ordinances of the churches of Christ.

Christ instituted the ordinance. Matthew 26:26-28 says: "And as they were eating, Jesus took bread, and blessed it, and brake it, and gave it to the disciples, and said, Take, eat; this is my body. And he took the cup, and gave thanks, and gave it to them, saying, Drink ye all of it; for this is my blood of the new testament [covenant], which is shed for many for the remission of sins." Paul, writing "unto the church of God which is at Corinth," says: "For I have received of the Lord that which also I delivered unto you. That the Lord Jesus the same night in which he was betrayed took bread: and when he had given thanks, he brake it, and said, Take, eat: this is my body, which is broken for you: this do in remembrance of me. After the same manner also he took the cup, when he had supped, saying, This cup is the new testament [covenant] in my blood: this do ye, as oft as ye drink it, in remembrance of me. For as often as ye eat this bread, and drink this cup, ye do shew the Lord's death till he come" (1 Cor. 11:23-26).

Surely any seeker after truth can know the design of the Lord's Supper. Baptists believe it is to commemorate the sufferings and death of our Lord Jesus Christ. He said: "This do in remembrance of me." "This do ye, as oft as ye drink it, in remembrance of me."

If only we keep in mind the object of the ordinance, it will save us from many errors concerning it. If we examine the popular notions of the present day, and listen to the unscriptural ideas that modern churches have propagated concerning it, the impressions are made that its main object is to show Christian love (sometimes envious hate) and liberality.

They say, "It is the Lord's table." Exactly so. Then he has the sole right to set forth the object of its observance, to fix the qualifications of its participants. Again they say: "We shall all commune together in heaven." Well, the object of the Lord's Supper is not our communing together here, but communing with Christ; not in remembrance of each other, for Jesus said "in remembrance of me."

Then, again, it is more than silly thus to speak. There will be no such ordinance in heaven. This is to be observed till he comes again, not *after* he comes. I submit, are not these things a perversion of the ordinance? Is not this eating, with these erroneous, unscriptural views, "not discerning the Lord's body"? Baptists believe it is. We believe it is to be sacredly kept "in remembrance" of him, "to shew the Lord's death till he come again." If you keep it with any other view, or with no recognition of this divine aim, you do not discern the Lord's body.

We are said to be peculiar in our views about this matter. Well, God's people are "a peculiar people"; so we are not worried about the charge brought against us. But are we very peculiar after all? Only in practice.

All those who use the term "close communion" as a cudgel to beat Baptists over the head, and to prejudice people against us, agree with us in theory, but have not the Christian manhood to be consistent in their practice.

Neander, the church historian, says of the Lord's Supper: "At this celebration, as may be easily concluded, no one could be present who was not a member of the Christian church, and incorporated into it by the rite of baptism."

Justin, martyr of the second century, wrote: "It is not lawful for any one to partake, but such as believe the things taught by us, and have been baptized."

Bishop Coxe (Episcopalian) says: "The Baptists hold that we have never been baptized, and they must exclude us from their communion table, if we were disposed to go there. Are we offended? No. We call it *proper* and we respect it.

"To say we have never become members of Christ by baptism seems severe, but if it is conscientious adherence to duty as they regard it, I should be a bigot, and not they, if I should ask them to violate their discipline in this or any other particular" (*Church Union,* July, 1891). Allow a word of comment upon this lengthy quotation.

Notice he says: "Become members of Christ by baptism." Yet some cannot be made to believe they teach baptismal regeneration. Some Episcopalians even, in ignorance of their own doctrine, deny it. Yet the prayer book could not well be plainer on this point. Again he says: "If we were disposed to go there.". Which of course they are not. Many of them, especially strict churchmen, would no more attend services at a Baptist, Methodist, or Presbyterian church than would a Roman Catholic. They have neither church fellowship nor Christian Fellowship for any who do not belong to the church established in the sixteenth century by Henry VIII. Yet I have known two young ladies who left a Baptist church and joined the Episcopal, saying they made the change because they did not believe in restricted communion. I know not whether to lay it to ignorance or hypocrisy. They evidently thought it more "tony" to belong to the Episcopal church. And yet many never think of the Episcopalians being retricted communionists because forsooth our pedobaptist friends never cudgel them for it.

Listen what the prayer book says on this point. Here is the law: "And there shall none be admitted to the holy communion until such time as he be confirmed, or be ready and desirous to be confirmed."

So Episcopalians in both theory and practice are restricted communionists.

The Methodist Discipline says: "No person shall be admitted to the Lord's Supper among us who is guilty of any practice for which we would exclude a member of our church." —Sec. 408. Every Methodist preacher takes a solemn vow, or oath, to obey his superiors and the discipline. Furthermore, this iron law of Methodism requires that they shall exclude from membership a man guilty of "inveighing against their doctrine or discipline."—Sec. 283. Or "who hold or disseminate, publicly or privately, doctrines which are contrary to our articles of religion."

So, in theory at least, no Methodist has a scintilla of liberality to boast about on this question. He should not want any such hypocritical liberality. He cannot have it and be true to his vow of subordination to his discipline and earthly lords. And, according to his discipline, there is not a true Baptist in the world prepared or allowed to come to his communion.

Presbyterian scholarship and the theory of the Presbyterian church is the same. Drs. Doddridge, Schaff, and Cuyler all occupy the Baptist position on this question.

Dr. John Dick, Presbyterian, says: "An uncircumcized man was not permitted to eat the passover, and an unbaptized man should not be permitted to partake of the eucharist." Again, "Baptism is requisite to entitle a person to a seat at the table of the Lord."—*Dick's Theology,* p. 421.

Congregationalists say the same.

Dr. Griffin, one of the most eminent divines of America, says: "I agree with the advocates of close communion . . . that we ought not to commune with those who have not been baptized, and of course are not church members, even if we regard them as Christians."

Quotations might be multiplied at pleasure, but this is enough to satisfy all inquirers after truth that Baptist and all so-called evangelical churches are agreed in theory.

Until they can adduce some proof that infant sprinkling is Bible baptism, let them cease their unjust criticism of restricted communion.

As already shown, all those who inveigh so much against "close communion" are really close communionists themselves.

Really, so far as I know, everybody who has any definite idea about the matter at all, believes in restricting the ordinance.

There is not an evangelical society or church in the world, I suppose, who believes everybody, without any regard to character or conduct, should participate with them in the Lord's Supper.

No one claims that infidels, scoffers, and the vile of earth should come to the table. "Oh," you say, "of course we do not mean that any who are not Christians should come." Then many of our church members of all denominations are excluded. But you say, they claim to be Christians, and you quote Paul and say, "Let a man examine himself, and so let him eat." But you misapply the Scripture, for Paul was writing to a local church, "the church of God which is at Corinth."

This is good scriptural advice to give a church, but it does not apply indiscriminately to everyone who might upon some ground claim to be a Christian.

Again, you may claim that all Christians should be invited. Well, who is to judge whether or not they are Christians? They are to judge themselves, the advocate for open communion answers.

Then you have thrown down some of the barriers, and the Catholic, the Mormon, the Free-thinker, the Communist, the Unitarian, and the Universalist are all invited to participate with you. You recoil from your own logic, or at least ought to, at the bare thought of such sacrilegious mockery. Then you say we mean to restrict it to evangelical Christians. Well, then you are getting to be quite a close communionist. Out of the hundreds of societies claiming to be Christians, you narrow it down to less than a half dozen with whom you are willing to commune. But again I ask, Who is to judge whether they are evangelical or not? You are judging that. Don't you see you are a restricted communionist?

Even some Baptists (?) claim to be open communionists.

When I was pastor at Russellville, Kentucky, I had a conversation with an old gentleman about as follows: Said I, "Are you a Christian?" He answered, "I hope so. Yes, I am a Christian, and have been for thirty years."

I said, "Well, I understand you have never united with any church, and none of your family are church members. Did you ever think that your derelictions of duty perhaps account for the irreligious condition of your family?" He answered, "Yes." "Well, what is the matter? Can't you find a church good enough for you to live in?" "That," said he, "is not the trouble. I think I am unworthy to be in any of them." I then asked, "What do you believe? What are your views of a church?" He answered, "I suppose I can say I am a Baptist in belief. I believe in repentance and faith and conversion. I believe immersion is the only baptism known or authorized in the New Testament. There is one thing which you believe which I do not, and that is your close communion." I said, "Oh, well, what is your idea of the ordinance?" He answered, "I do not believe your close communion is right." To draw him out, I said, "Do you think these Methodists and Presbyterians are Christians?" With a look of surprise, he said, "Certainly I do. Don't you?" I answered, "I certainly do." "Then," said he, "if they are Christians, they have as much right to come to the communion table as you, and you have no right to exclude them. It is the Lord's table, and they are his people." "You place it then upon the ground of being a Christian; that is your only prerequisite to the Lord's Supper?" "Certainly," he answered, "all Christians should come." I said, "Have you ever partaken of the Lord's Supper?" "I? No, no, I would not think of such a thing. I would not do such a thing for my right arm." I said, "Why not? You claim to be a Christian?" He said, with apparent alarm, "But I have never been baptized. No, no, I could not do such a thing. I have never been baptized." I said, "Well, have these whom you are so anxious to have invited to participate in this ordinance been baptized? According to your expressed belief they have not, and yet you are anxious for them to do what you would not do for your right arm."

Here was an intelligent man kept out of the church for thirty years because he did not believe in restricted communion, thought all Christians should partake of the Lord's Supper, that to be a Christian was the only prerequisite, and yet when he applied his reasoning to his own case he shrank from the application of his logic. He was conscientious and sensible. As soon as he saw his error he abandoned it, and that very night came before the church and told his thirty-year-old experience and asked to be baptized.

Baptists believe that none are scripturally entitled to partake of the Lord's Supper except such as have made a credible profession of faith. This is plain enough if you mean to follow the examples of early Christians in the days of the apostles. At its institution none were present except those who were the professed disciples of Christ. On the day of Pentecost those who broke bread had first "gladly received the word."

The Greek Catholic Church observes infant communion along with infant baptism, and they use the same arguments for infant communion that are used in favor of infant baptism. There is no Scripture for either, and if you rely upon sentiment or the supposed saving efficacy of baptism, there is equal ground for infant communion. I had as soon administer the bread and wine to a dying baby as to sprinkle water upon it in the name of the Trinity and call it baptism. Everything in favor of believers' baptism is equally in favor of believers' communion.

Baptists believe that baptism properly precedes the Lord's Supper. Jesus gave the example. He was baptized at the beginning of his ministry, and instituted the Supper just prior to his death.

The Commission places baptism before communion and faith before baptism. "Go ye therefore, and teach [*i.e.*, disciple] all nations, baptizing them in the name of the Father, and of the Son, and of the Holy Ghost: teaching them to observe all things whatsoever I have commanded you." First, "make disciples," then baptize them, then observe all things commanded. The Lord's Supper is one of the things commanded, and to be observed after the believer has become a disciple and been baptized as such.

The apostles so understood and practiced. On the day of Pentecost, in case of Saul, the jailer, Lydia, etc.

Baptists believe church membership is also a prerequisite to the Lord's Supper.

Paul, writing to the "church of God which is at Corinth," said, "I received of the Lord that which I also delivered unto you," certainly "unto the church." There is no scriptural authority for carrying the emblems around to sick people, and administering in any case except by the church. It was delivered to the church at Corinth, and just as surely to the church at Ephesus, the church in Jerusalem, etc.

Let us look a moment now at this from a scriptural standpoint. Here is the command and example of Christ, the practice of the apostles, the clear light of Scripture; now, as the servants of Christ, can we dare for the sake of sentiment, or the approbation of those walking disorderly, to violate the plain teachings of God's Word?

Pedobaptists can invite us to commune with them, for they acknowledge our baptism as scriptural and right, and we do not believe they have been baptized at all, hence are not authorized by the Word of God to administer the ordinance or to partake of it. Yet there are inconsistencies in their invitation to us, but not because we have not been baptized, they being the judges.

Suppose I go to a Methodist church with a Methodist preacher, they give their usual invitation, I am included in it, accept it, and am heartily welcomed. They would publish it from Dan to Beersheba. Suppose the next Sunday I preach a sermon in my pulpit, I prove from the Scriptures that immersion is the only scriptural baptism, the scriptural form of church government is that vested in a local church, that when a soul has obtained eternal life by faith in Christ, that soul has eternal life and will reach heaven because it is saved, etc. Now what will be the result if the Methodist preacher preaches the same scriptural truths? He would be tried, his papers taken from him, and he excluded. Now suppose a month later we go to the same church again, and when the invitation is given, he is left out and I am included. Why? Am I in harmony with Methodism any more than he? Let pedobaptists quit taking such vows as their disciplines, confessions, etc., impose, or else quit breaking these vows, and posing as liberalists in order to curry favor with the world.

Baptists believe in God, in his authority, his wisdom, his infallible word. They do not believe any mortal has the right to add to, or take from, "the things which are written" therein.

CHAPTER XVII
Missions

Baptists believe in missions. Every Christian, in every legitimate way, all the time, everywhere, according to ability, ought to seek to spread a knowledge of Jesus and the way of salvation.

No one can be a true Baptist who has not repented of sin, trusted in Jesus, and him alone, for life and salvation, and seeks to know and do the will of his divine Lord.

Some of the important commands of Jesus are: "Repent and believe the gospel." "Believe in me." "Follow me," "Let your light shine." "Let him that heareth say come." "Go ye therefore, and teach all nations." "Go ye into all the world and preach the gospel." "Keep my commandments." We, as Baptists have been great sticklers and advocates for the maintenance of the ordinances, and church policy as set forth in the Scriptures; keeping the ordinances as they were delivered unto us, and maintaining the form of government established by Christ and the apostles, seeking to execute the laws divinely given. This we ought to have done, and we ought not to have neglected the other. The same Lord who invites all men to come, commands all men to repent, requires all men to believe, and commands all believers to be baptized, and all baptized believers to observe the Lord's Supper, in remembrance of him till he comes again, also and equally commands that all his followers shall "Go ye into all the world and preach the gospel to every creature." "Teach all nations," to be witnesses for him to the uttermost part of the earth. Neglecting these things, will he not say, "Why call ye me Lord, Lord and do not the things which I say?" Do you love him? He says, "If ye love me, keep my commandments."

Will you be an unfaithful servant, knowing your duty and doing it not, and be beaten with many stripes; or a faithful servant of whom he shall say, Ye have done what ye could? Remember, he says, "Be thou faithful even unto death, and I will give thee a crown of life."